RENAISSANCE

Amy Clennell

Amy Clennell

ABOUT THE AUTHOR

Amy Clennell has cerebral palsy, and she uses a wheelchair. She also has hidden disabilities, including severe dyspraxia and its associated anxiety problems; she is partially sighted as well. Because of the latter, she can't see well enough to read, and because of the former, she cannot read Braille, type or write. She relies on others to be her eyes and hands.

Nevertheless, Amy graduated from Coventry University in 2007 with a degree in theatre and professional practice. She has led drama workshops for both adults and children with disabilities. And she has taken to writing in recent years, publishing short stories and poems, and self-publishing her first book in 2014.

RENAISSANCE

Amy Clennell

Cherish
EDITIONS

First published in Great Britain 2022 by Cherish Editions
Cherish Editions is a trading style of Shaw Callaghan Ltd & Shaw Callaghan 23 USA, INC.
The Foundation Centre
Navigation House, 48 Millgate, Newark
Nottinghamshire NG24 4TS UK
www.triggerhub.org
Text Copyright © 2022 Amy Clennell

All rights reserved. No part of this publication may be reproduced, stored in a retrieval system, or transmitted in any form or by any means, electronic, mechanical, photocopying, recording or otherwise, without prior permission in writing from the publisher

British Library Cataloguing in Publication Data
A CIP catalogue record for this book is available upon request from the British Library
ISBN: 978-1-913615-58-1
This book is also available in the following eBook formats:
ePUB: 978-1-913615-59-8

Amy Clennell has asserted her right under the Copyright, Design and Patents Act 1988 to be identified as the author of this work

Cover design by Kitty Turner
Typeset by Lapiz Digital Services

All artwork within the book comes from the following creators on iStock by Getty Images:

taylan_ozgur • Tetiana Garkusha • Andrii Koltun • prezent • Retany • Tetiana Kiichenko • ByM • sliplee • lumyaisweet • HearttoHeart0225 • Jobalou • Gwens Graphic Studio • Mykola Lishchyshyn • samuii • Aleksey Eremin • AlenaChe • bankapollo • Vitalii Barida • Iryna Sydorchuk • Fourleaflover • Burocx • yugoro • undefined undefined

For my family and my friend Iaine

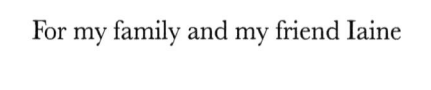

TABLE OF CONTENTS

Morwenna	1
Ready to Fly	2
Sisterly Love	4
Blessed	5
My Alfie	6
Haiku #1	7
The Elephant in the Classroom, "Special School", Coundon	8
Fringe of the Grove in Sunlight	10
Salvage	11
Sunflower Seeds of Hope	12
The Jovial Jibes of the Swing	13
A Tragedy in Floriography	14
The Launderer's Lament	15
Sacrifice	17
Eglantine	18
A Gothic Romance	19
The Red Shoes	20
Courage and Kindness	21
Duel at Dawn	22
Postmortem	23
Lesson Learnt	24
A Modern Troubadour	26
Haiku #2	27
Hope for Winter, a Story of Dolphins	28
Evelyn Rose	30
In My Fairy Glen	31
Backyard Critters	32
Fat Club	33
Limericks	34

Haiku #3	35
An Unkindness of Ravens	36
Something to Do With Cake	38
Haiku #4	39
Sometimes the Grass is Greener	41
What a Pantomime	42
Renaissance	43
Acknowledgements	45

MORWENNA

When people look at me
What do they see?
Perfectly formed from head to waist,
Rigid legs protruding like a mermaid's tail,
With no display of shimmering scales.
In the water I am free.
I am no mythical creature,
Merely a human being,
Vulnerable, yet not wishing to conform.
Underestimated or overrated?
Undeterred, I swim without ceasing
Toward the shore and uncertain sanctuary.
Some glance on the sly as I glide by,
While others with gaping mouths gawp.
Does anyone hear my siren call?
I should disregard patronage, spite and violation.
Still their debris pollutes the shore
To belittle achievement and happiness.
I am who I am.
This is me.

READY TO FLY

When I arrive, Linda takes me for a wash.
I like her, she's fun. I never see her frown.
I get clean clothes while mine go in the machine.
And breakfast!
I have my hair brushed.
And Linda takes ages with that little comb.
It pulls a bit but not like at home
When Mummy yanks a handful to drag me along.

I've made lots of friends.
At school we play together all day
But soon it's time to clear away.
I don't want to go back.
Back to smacks and slaps,
Snarling mouth telling me I'm a stupid bitch.
Another beating. No more eating.

What have I done?
I try to speak like they can but you never
understand.
My world is silent. Still, I see your angry face
As I search your eyes for the slightest trace
Of love.

Now I live with a new family.
Temporarily.
My own bed! Baths and a toothbrush,
New clothes and plenty of food.
No harsh words or bruises.
Even though they are kind-hearted
I know quite soon we will be parted.

It's our school sports day. I'm leading the race.
I look behind me and quicken my pace
The crowd cheer and applaud though no parent
To spur me on.
But I am not defeated although the road is long.
I look ahead to the finish line and know
I must stay strong.

Multicoloured collage bird.
We add pieces, one by one,
Until finally it's done.
Now it's going on display
With wings spread to fly away.

SISTERLY LOVE

I always wanted a sister.
Together we would play with our dolls
or dress up as princesses
in Mum's old summer dresses and wear tinsel tiaras.
Maybe we would be fairies, flitting over the flowers
or twirling ballerinas on our green lawn stage.
Of course, at first she would be too small, Sophie Claire,
but she would soon grow.
And if it was a boy, I would send it back
because what I wanted was a sister.
Then one Thursday Mum went in for her "ceasarium".
In the afternoon the piercing tone of the telephone
punctured the calm of story time.
The beaming Mrs Liney handed me the receiver.
"I've got a little brother!"
Like a rabbit from a hat, my teacher produced
a Victoria Sandwich.
We all had a slice.
He was sleeping like Snow White in a glass coffin.
His gown was pale blue with a white daisy motif,
a hospital band around his wrist.
Smelling of Johnson's baby lotion,
Cradling him in my arms, much better than any doll,
I kissed him.
He opened his blue eyes
and gazed up into mine.
Hello Stuart *Christopher*,
I chose *that* name.
As he gripped my finger in his tiny hand
I knew that he would always hold my heart.

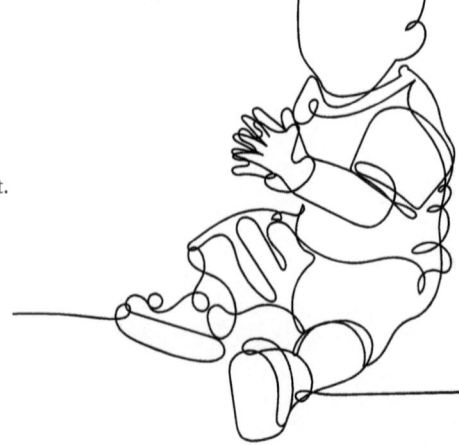

BLESSED

Our duet together, remembered forever.
Guests like guppies gawping at the game girl.
Is this karma then, like you once said, Glenn?

Cripples in the front row, so where else should they go?
Spastics like shit shovelled into the shadows.
And now they are gone, more impressions, John?

Audience is in a rage – where's the star, he's not on stage?
Veterans vowed not to vacate the vanguard.
Hope you never lose a limb, you might consider that, Jim.

So first I spoke with you, with the glamorous two,
previous promises perjured perfunctorily.
Knew you were only his paid lackey, and I could smell the wacky baccy!

In the end I met Lemar, my illuminating star!
With gentle gestures, both genuine and generous,
your stardom was at its height, but to me, my gallant knight.

No well-rehearsed band as you held my hand,
our melody mellowing the maelstrom of memories.
We both had faith, we both had trust, that moment was all about us.
Now I can ignore the rest because you said you were blessed.

MY ALFIE

My son and I reside
In adjacent spheres
Which often may collide
If I don't adhere
To rigid rituals.

It's hard to comprehend
Why peace is shattered.
My task is to transcend
The debris scattered
By his relentless rage.

Like two globes gliding by
Closely yet remote
Or bubbles in the sky
Side by side we float
In silent solitude.

His world is so lonely,
Mine he cannot share.
How I wish, if only
I could place in there
Just one fragile foothold.

I might see through his eyes,
Glance into his mind.
A chance to empathize
If our thoughts combined,
Shine through this hopeless haze.

He can hear, he can speak,
Yet he's thought witless.
He's even called a freak
By those who witness
His bizarre behaviour.

And often they complain
About his loud shouts
Once more I must explain
Though they have their doubts,
"Alfie is autistic."

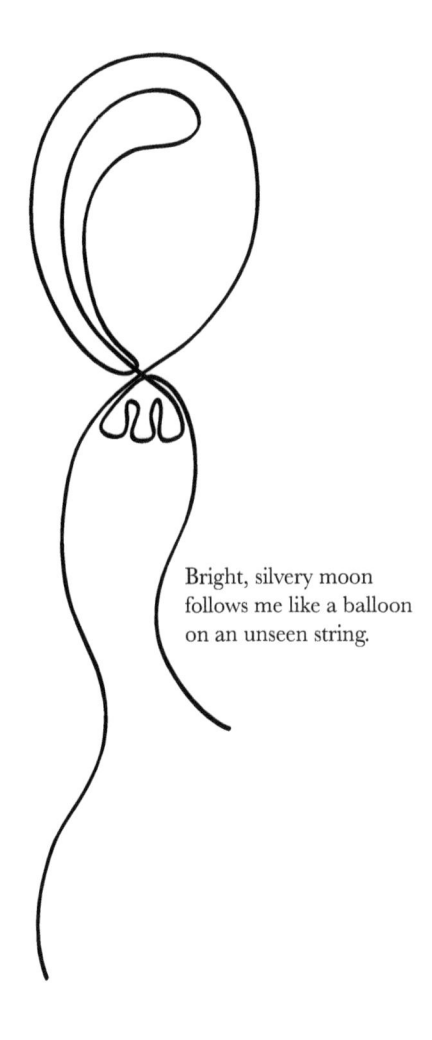

Bright, silvery moon
follows me like a balloon
on an unseen string.

THE ELEPHANT IN THE CLASSROOM, "SPECIAL SCHOOL", COUNDON.

Today would be your forty-first birthday.
We were both so young but you
remain forever sixteen.

Yet, I wonder, where you are.
Do you live again in Coventry?
Or do you now bathe in the holy Ganges?
You are not alone.
Do you see the others,
as I do?
Are you with your brother who left before you?

From infants we grew
alongside those who were able
to leap, dance and sing.
We watched too their decline,
those condemned to shrinking lives,
to fall still and silent,
like nurtured orchids.
We did not witness each floret fall,
merely the vacant space in the vase.

And, like them, for you there appeared no invigorating beacon,
but you continued on your journey.
Perhaps it is as well that you did not stay
for today you would be serving out your sentence in
solitary confinement.
For some, life's train stopped briefly
at every station.
Some were victims of violent derailment.
A few, though clutching high-speed tickets,
still took the slower train.
All ultimately to arrive at their
inevitable destination.

It came not as a sudden realization.
Cognizance gradually grew
like shadows as dusk approaches.
We acknowledged those selected,
not rejected,
accepted,
and of equal worth.

Daily we ignored the predator posed to pounce,
until, in the morning, once more the train
pulled into the station.
The head teacher boarded our compartment,
our unwavering gaze upon her,
as the benevolent smile faded from her lips;
that familiar expression of suppressed melancholy
before she dutifully delivered her grim tidings;
another of our fellow passengers had disembarked.
There followed tears, consoling cuddles and sweet tea
and reminiscences
before our journey continued on...
to the next standstill.

One morning I awoke with no tangible portent,
but a sense of foreboding.
I knew I had lost you, my
intelligent,
gentle
kind,
supportive
friend.
And in my musings, we still dance to that same melody.

In memory of:
Deepak, Manish, Colin, Safda, Sarah H, Sarah W, Ben, Lisa, Paul C, Paul G, Scott,
Chris T, Chris F, Ashish, Johnathan, Michael T, Michael Th, Graham, James, Gary,
Anna, Zoe, Andrew, Kelly, Brian and Amina.

FRINGE OF THE GROVE IN SUNLIGHT

At the kiss of a zephyr the ocean

of Queen Anne's lace is transformed

to a rolling mist from which

rise oaken limbs, towering

regally over their subjects.

And birds-eye, like fallen flakes of cerulean sky,

throng, gazing wistfully toward a lost heaven.

SALVAGE

Bound by the lure of The Lorelei,
Seduced by the siren song,
I looked on as,
With hull smashed like an eggshell,
The vessel spewed out its essence.
Fleeting sepulchral spaces
Devoured by an insatiable sea.
Now those final futile cries resound
In my ear,
Above wailing gale and moaning ocean.
And the taking of those lives so forcibly
Spared my own.

SUNFLOWER SEEDS OF HOPE

Bearing her leaves, like hearts on sleeves,
Clytie awaits the Sun God's kiss
She lifts her face, seeking his grace,
in vain hope of a lovers' tryst.
She casts her eyes toward the skies,
enraptured by his perfect mien.
There was a time their souls entwined,
too soon another came between.
His passion waned while she remains
serenely patient, ever true.
To win His love, she bides above
'til her life in this realm is through.
> Yet from 'neath the earth springs Clytie's rebirth,
> destined to follow her own Apollo.

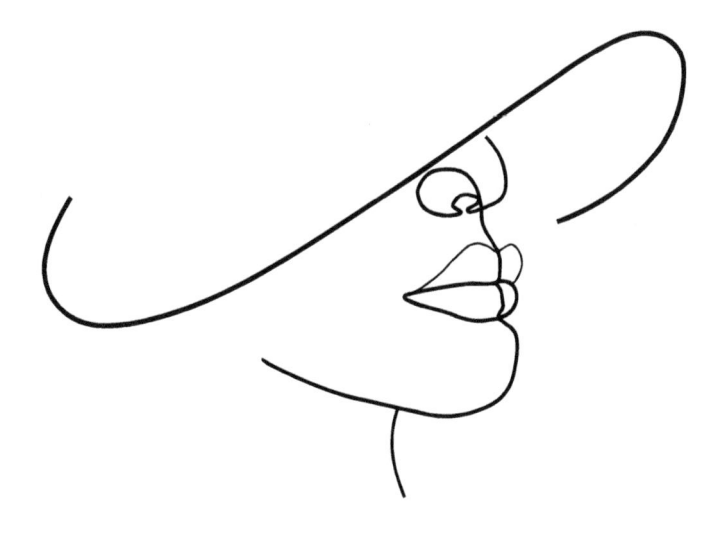

THE JOVIAL JIBES OF THE SWING
Inspired by the painting *The Swing* (1767)
by Jean-Honore Fragonard

The cuckold clasps my reins
as disdainfully I rise ever
higher in the eyes of my swain.
To and fro I flow.
And Cupid and l'escarpolette
conspire in my coquetry,
as I cast off my shoe in
mockery of this beau below
who savours this halcyon day,
assuming my favours are assured,
incognizant of my other secret
paramour.

A TRAGEDY IN FLORIOGRAPHY
Inspired by the painting *Ophelia* (1851-2)
by John Everett Millais

Beneath the willow lies forsaken love,
Ne'er more enduring pain of nettles' sting.
Entombed within a fragrant floral grove,
Now flowers tell the tale her lips can't sing.
The pansy and the meadowsweet expose
How hollow is the heart that loves in vain.
And misused love despoils the comely rose
Who learns how fleet is lust to wax and wane.
Though daisies three proclaim her innocence,
A chain of violets foretells her fate;
To suffer early death for no offence
Since loosestrife's peaceful pardon comes too late.
    Fritillary does not her woe belie,
    Such sorrow borne out in the pheasant's eye.

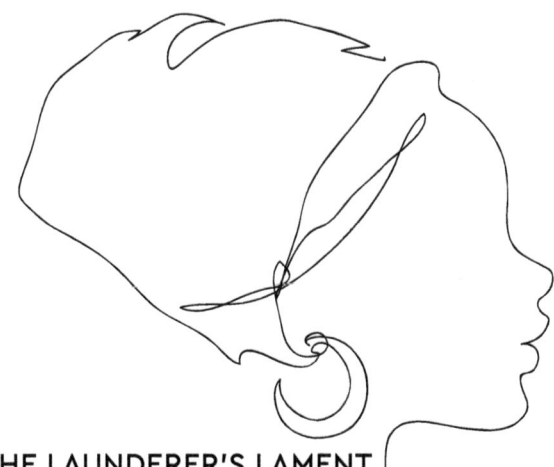

THE LAUNDERER'S LAMENT
Inspired by the painting
Women Ironing (1884) by Edgar Degas

We two women toil side by side,
Labouring from dawn until dark.
My exhaustion I cannot hide,
I was awake before the lark.
How I wish our work was complete
So I could rest my aching feet.

Would that this bottle still held wine,
Then she and I might take a pause.
Some bread and cheese would suit us fine
But we must press on with our chores.
Stifling our hunger and our thirst,
To lives of drudgery we're cursed.

My companion is quite robust,
Heaving that iron to and fro.
Although her strength I do not mistrust,
I'll tell you something, this I know,
To flatten that remaining crease,
She will need much more elbow grease.

Though smoothing sheets is backbreaking,
This work is shared, you realize.
Hard slog but there's no mistaking,
It's those toffs' shirts I despise.
If I have to starch one more cuff,
I'll tell you now, I've had enough.

16

SACRIFICE
Inspired by the short story "The Happy Prince"
by Oscar Wilde

Looking down upon the city,
azure eyes awash with pity,
the gilded prince of golden leaf
views the hardship in disbelief.

The swallow rests on his search for warmer weathers.
It is not rain that falls upon his soft feathers,
but tears of a restless spirit, without release,
who must give his folk hope to find his inner peace.

Oh, little swallow, pray do as I bid,
for all sickness from that boy I would rid.
Pry the crimson ruby from my sword's hilt,
give him the riches and assuage my guilt.

Take both of my sapphire eyes, pluck them free.
The writer is shivering and hungry.
The girl's matches are spilled, I see her plight.
Neither shall die with the gift of my sight.

Strip away my sumptuous skin of gold,
I am not deterred by the freezing cold.
My people need these riches more than I,
your work complete, soar now into the sky.

Alas my dear prince it is not to be.
No more time on this earth is left to me.
My heart in unison with yours may break
yet you revered prince I will not forsake.

The great King of all says, "Complete this task,
two most precious items are what I ask.
This leaden heart, forever strong and free,
with this small bird shall sing praises to me."

EGLANTINE
Inspired by the painting
Young Man Among Roses (1587)
by Nicholas Hilliard

This heart was once a songbird on the wing
Which soared to heights beyond this Earthly sphere.
Alas, this bird no more may ever sing
For Paradise is lost since you're not near.
My love remains as steadfast as the oak
Which withers not but grows in strength each day,
With roots so deep my passion to evoke.
Our veiled affaire de coeur I'll ne'er betray.
Though petals fall to drift upon the breeze,
Sweet Eglantine, your fragrance lingers yet.
Mere memories do not my soul appease,
Abandoned, still unable to forget.
    And now your wounding barbs are so revealed,
      Tis clear this punctured heart may ne'er be healed.

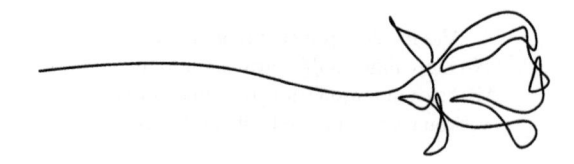

A GOTHIC ROMANCE
Inspired by Matthew Bourne's
Sleeping Beauty ballet

Aurora, since the darkness sends forth dawn.
Good Fairy Folk grant peerless attributes.
Oh woe, now she bestows her hex with scorn.
Tis Royal gratitude that's in dispute.
Hence Count of Lilac intervenes in time,
Ill-fated child in slumber you shall lie.
Could commoner and princess hearts entwine?
Remember yet that curse of years gone by.
On thorn of blackest rose her finger torn,
Macabre mystique impels her dormant state.
Alas her secret love is left forlorn,
Neath bite of living death which seals his fate.
      Cadaverous he kisses his true bride,
      Ere long as other worldly they abide.

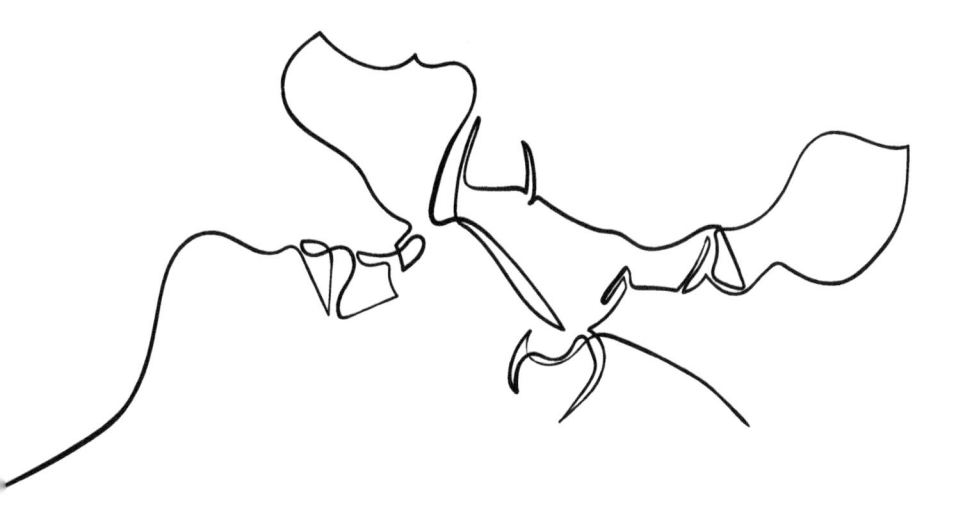

THE RED SHOES
Inspired by the film *The Red Shoes*

The master orders me to give him up,
There cannot be two passions in my life.
I am presented with a poisoned cup,
His words slash through my heart just as a knife.
Are you the very devil at my feet,
Compelling me to dance for evermore?
Without my lover I am incomplete,
Giselle or Carmen with no music score.
Your scarlet tentacles clutch at my soul
Which seeks serenity but sees no dove.
Eternally you constantly cajole,
So how shall I resolve this tug-of-love?
    With hiss of steam oppressive in my head
    Farewell *amours* my choice is death instead.

COURAGE AND KINDNESS
Inspired by the film *Cinderella*

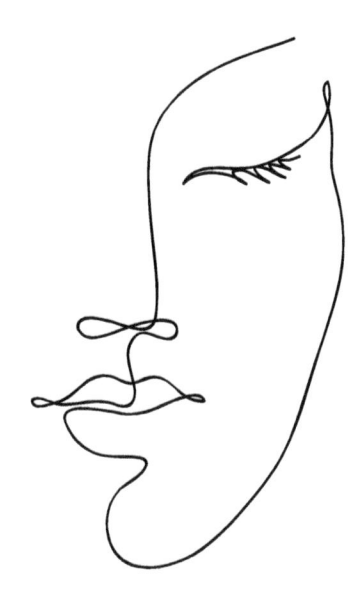

As I step out of this drudgery into fine satins,
the bedraggled waif in rags and tatters
is no more.
Wooden clogs replaced by sparkling silver slippers of spun glass.
My face, no longer tarnished by ashes and soot,
now glows radiantly.
Is this an illusion or reality;
This wish held in my heart like a butterfly
freed from ensnarement?
Yet will this feeling last
or will it be as the smoke of a snuffed out flame,
consumed by darkness?
Only the angels in Heaven know.
I will live for this moment,
whatever the future brings,
as I recall my parents' words,
"Hold fast to courage and kindness."

DUEL AT DAWN

Grazing on flaxen scrub beyond the river,

horse ignores cockerel's call to arms.

In the chill breeze bare-stemmed grasses quail and quiver,

fleeing squirrel intensifies their qualms.

Birch trees loom like predators, shoulder to shoulder,

stripped of their seasonal resplendence.

Verdant, waving firs warn them, become no bolder,

for winter signals our ascendance.

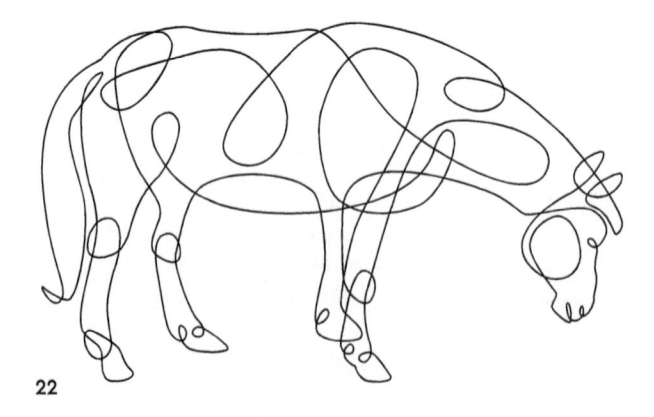

POSTMORTEM

I am here to tell you, Mary,
On this dark and fearsome night,
How I came to know you.

We are face to face there and I think, "OMG"
I don't want a confrontation.
I turn to escape the loathing in your glare,
But you just grab and push me...
                             backwards.

I am cast down the cold stairs.
You decide my fate.
You leave me to bleed, to fade from consciousness,
With blank, staring eyes.

Now you must know the soul endures.
The murdered linger, ever restless,
Lifeless eyes reflecting all.

LESSON LEARNT

Beyond the "NO SWIMMING" sign,
loitering low in the lagoon,
skulking, silent, still;
a sudden lurch, oblivious prey snatched from the shore.

A chilling veil of horror, disbelief enshrouds.
Animated faces are distorted, bodies petrified by
the gruesome scene like one from *Jaws* or *Jurassic Park*.
Not the anticipated Disney family movie.

Gasps, screams, running feet flick up the sand.
The frantic father wrestles with its mouth
his hands blooded by the unyielding, saw-like teeth.
The reptile thrashes and breaks free.

The beast glides gracefully away,
pauses, impassive, before slowly submerging,
prey firmly gripped.
Incredulous eyes scan the tranquil water; nothing further to witness.

Tomorrow the toddler's corpse is recovered,
small solace that it is intact.
Restrictive boulders strategically placed.
Fresh signage warning of predators.

A MODERN TROUBADOUR

His father wrenched away,
his older siblings seeping into marital agreements,
he resolved to flow downstream,
guitar slung over one shoulder
like Whittington's bundle on a stick.

Was he seduced by notions of gilded streets
as he surged on a southerly course?

Any qualms allayed,
the aspiring minstrel sang and
played never straying from this channel.

Until
enthusiasm faded as
homeless, homesick, jaded,
he meandered,
guitar slung over one shoulder
like a hobo with his bindle.

Clear, blue skies, sunshine,
vibrant rainbow hues revealed
within water spray.

HOPE FOR WINTER, A STORY OF DOLPHINS
Inspired by the films *A Dolphin Tale* and *A Dolphin Tale 2*

Out in the great, wide ocean, so much to explore,
Full of energy and exuberance, streaking through the depths,
Exploding from the waves, I reached for the azure heights.
Basking in the sun's rays, chattering with my family,
All greeting the passing vessels, before off we go,
Leaping in unison, we were joyful in our freedom.
But curiosity led me astray,
No companions on that fateful day.

This was not a friend, although it held me in its grasp.
Possessed by fright and panic, I struggled to break free.
With all my power I endeavoured to escape,
Jerking, swishing, writhing, wrenching, still the ligature remained taut.
Desperate, exhausted, vanquished, forlorn, my frantic cries unheard,
The calm serenity of the lagoon reigned once more as my efforts ceased.
My captor made no hostile sound
And yet I remained firmly bound.

A cacophony of distant voices kindled my senses.
Alas, not my sweet mother's call, but familiar still.
I recognized the shouts of the land creatures.
Skilfully their hands freed me from ensnarement.
I felt the comfort of their touch as fingers tenderly caressed me.
Their words, whispered in kindly tone, sustained my spirit.
And as those gentle hands raised me up from the sea.
I knew both relief and fear in my liberty.

My new friends nursed and nourished me from near death to recovery.
Their constant compassion and care confirmed my resolve.
Even as my tail fell away, piece by piece,
I remained steadfast in my desire to survive.
My health regained I was apprehensive in my anticipation.
But all trepidation evanesced as the waters and I embraced.
Now reconciled I glided through my man-made sea,
My broken body not perfect but I was me.

Instinctively moving myself laterally,
I played alongside my companion Panama.
We spent many contented hours in empathy.
Then one day a device was fastened where my tail should be.
Unsure I ventured cautiously and, elated, I swam naturally!
For brief interludes each day my temporary tail became part of me.
But life's tranquillity was not to last,
Confirmed once more when my only friend passed.

Overwhelmed in my grief, silently I lamented.
In my solitary situation, within my diminished world,
My melancholy dwelt upon my bodily inhibitions.
As I plunged deeper toward my desolate destination,
My life force pleaded to persevere, and the ascent began.
Now we spiral upwards together, my new playmate Hope and I…
And you would see, should you visit us today,
All anguish and sadness have melted away.

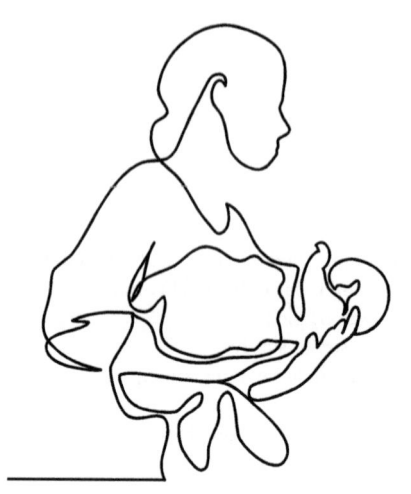

EVELYN ROSE

Amid the pandemic a surprise arrival,
a gift delivered hastily by hand,
yet with such tenuous prospects of survival,
her life suspended on a slender strand.
    Evelyn Rose determined to strive.
Anxious minutes extended into hours, days, nights,
as swathed in love this cherished child endured.
Expertise and vigilance foremost in her fight,
her future with her family ensured.
    Evelyn Rose continued to strive.
Very soon this precious rosebud began to bloom,
petals unfolding to reveal her worth.
Now her delightful smile illuminates the room.
Who knows what treasures still to be unearthed,
    as Evelyn Rose continues to thrive?

To quote J M Barrie, "To live will be an awfully big adventure."

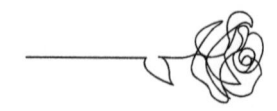

IN MY FAIRY GLEN

I inspected the peacock and tortoiseshell butterflies
Fluttering against the satin-white rose,
Unlike us stomping dinosaurs that we were.
Yet I wasn't a monster; still a little scrap of a thing.

Taking control of myself, I heaved my stiff body from the chair.
I set my sights on the shelter of leaves far away;
A half dozen steps and my aching joints
Could bear no more.

The stinging salty tears rolled down my cheeks.
She dabbed my face and hushed me,
"Be very quiet, we're close to a nest of fairies. Look!
There's one now."

I saw only a butterfly and stared at her,
Wondering if she could see something I could not.
My face was hot. I closed my eyes
And in that moment I felt them all around me.

Silvery specks sitting on the purple pansies
And so, step by step, I reached the end of the garden.
They shone in the shady glen
And I wished that they would heal my tired body.

That would never be
But they healed my tired soul.
And to this day
Walking has never been as draining.

Now Great Aunt and Uncle are gone.
Someone new lives there
But the fairies will always remain to help,
Whenever needed.

BACKYARD CRITTERS

His head is like a nodding donkey,
Sped up.
Fervently he forages for food.
Perhaps I could creep closer,
Quietly,
Since his eyesight is not good?
Armadillo's body is
Segmented like a woodlouse.
I'm rumbled! He scurries off
Like a giant clockwork mouse.

Slyly the submarine surfaces,
Periscopic eyes
Scanning the shore.
Silently he glides toward his prey,
Surface graze healing in his wake.
But eagle-eyed egret flies away.
El-lagarto creeps from the lake
To catch some rays instead.

Hi there, baby snapping turtle!
Who have you come to see?
Should I return you to the lake
For alligator's tea?

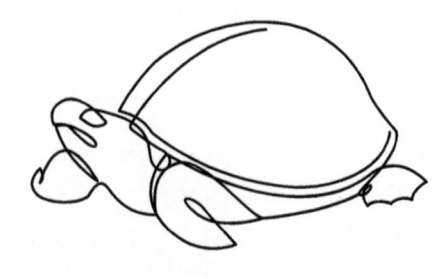

FAT CLUB

Salivating at the sight
and mmmm... that smell
of fried mozzarella sticks.
Eyes ogling the cranberry dip
as it drip, drips en route to lips.
Tempted to pounce.
But no! Resist.
Eyes down at my green leaf salad,
no dressing.

There was a young spaniel called Myrtle
Who oft' through the garden would hurtle.
    In a deep pond she fell
    And came up with a shell
'Cause a tortoise can't swim like a turtle.

        ***

I had a little bichon named Bertie
On his walks he got extremely dirty.
    When he started to stink
    I put him in the sink
And told him I'll be back at five – thirty.

        ***

I had a black Labrador called Sally
Who was always completely doolally.
    She chased her own tail
    Up hill and down dale
And finished with a poop in the valley.

Chilly winter morn.
Alpine blooms over the rocks
mimic a hoarfrost.

AN UNKINDNESS OF RAVENS

Security had been tightened.
Bags must not be left unattended.
Parked cars were viewed with suspicion.
It still seemed like only yesterday,
incredible images constantly recollected,
but the atrocity did really happen.
Annihilation of the monolithic structures
and the indiscriminate slaughter of everyday life,
less than half a year since.

Fearful thoughts of danger in our own city
had been banished.
On my way to Drury Lane,
traffic was horrendous, as always
but I'd forgotten my cosmetics.
The cabbie listened to my story.
It was okay, he'd got The Knowledge.
Eye shadow, mascara, foundation, blusher and lipstick,
all purchased, while he waited,
outside The Body Shop.
At the theatre he helped with my wheelchair
and cheerfully refusing payment,
wished me good luck.
"You're a gentleman," vouched my dad,
as Cabbie still declined the tenner
being pressed into his palm.

I entered another age of red velvet and gilded marquetry,
Surely royalty had once been frequent guests?
Rehearsal done, back to the hotel,
Only to return that evening in a limousine!
Lights and crowds and what's that, a camera?
The journalist pronounced that I would sing on TV.
Thank you, dreams come true!
Momentarily bemused, I blubbed.
Then, on with the show!

Alone in the spotlight, I sang out into the blackness
my song of love.
I was in orbit high above the dark skies,
No friendly face in the moon, no moon, no stars.
Tumultuous applause, a huge cuddly toy and an
exquisite bouquet of flowers returned me safely to precious Earth.

SOMETHING TO DO WITH CAKE

A sheen of blue frosting
covered the rocket-shaped red velvet,
a wedding cake for my brother
and his American-Filipino beauty.
She was perfection; dark hair a contrast with her white dress.
A Disney design for a fairy-tale ending,
with my brother in black playing the handsome prince.
They had brought me a souvenir from Paris;
miniature Eiffel Tower all sparkles and pink,
something they knew I'd be able to see.
Whenever I look at it, I picture them there
where he had asked and her answer was yes,
through happy tears.
Together they had fastened their love lock
to the Pont des Arts.
A year earlier, on a sweltering day at Universal Studios,
she'd been at work on the Rip Ride Rockit roller coaster.
He'd been making excuses to slip back to see her all day,
feeling a chance of love amidst his then-roller coaster life.
She helped him piece back his world as they built one for themselves.
We all saw it as they cut that whimsical cake
and took their first sweet bites.

Lest ill luck befalls,
leave the May tree to flourish.
Fairies' rendezvous.

SOMETIMES THE GRASS *IS* GREENER

Last week had been our first meeting,
Before that, we'd never conversed.
I'd caught glimpses, only fleeting,
Of his movements as he traversed
The meadow adjacent to mine.

The burgeoning bushes and trees
Have created a scenic screen;
Springtime presents a fragrant frieze,
As summer's verdure intervenes,
The density intensifies.

Autumn's palette transforms the hues
Of this effusive barricade.
Shedding of leaves slowly ensues,
Bared branches and twigs are displayed
Densely entwined throughout winter.

Did he observe these same tableaux
Each year as the seasons shifted?
The answer I would never know,
Unless this lush blockade lifted.
I wonder if he wonders too?

Then came the day a gap emerged,
A breach in the constraining wall.
Now were our meadows to be merged
Or were they about to install
A gate or another rampart?

Yet this open portal remained.
First we exchanged a friendly nod,
Then with our passage unrestrained,
Through each other's pastures we trod.
We became inseparable.

I am a grey, he is a bay.
Wherever he goes, I follow.
We graze together through the day,
We will do the same tomorrow
Safe in our equine paradise.

WHAT A PANTOMIME
Dedicated to Iain Lauchlan

The theatre lights go out,
Then resounds a "Hello!" shout.
That's The Dame, there is no doubt.
First she sports a cupcake dress,
Now a chandelier? Yes!
Next Eiffel Tower, I guess.
In garish make-up and gaudy attire,
To make folk laugh is her only desire.

RENAISSANCE

Oh Phoenix, glowing golden in the light
You soar above in fiery sunset sky.
Arise from ash; escape your fatal plight,
For truth and hope must surely never die.
From smould'ring cinders mystical rebirth,
Bedecked in gems your scarlet wings spread wide.
Come vanquish evil and its roots unearth,
Preserve the precious stones your plumage hides.
To you your splendour has no real import
Yet some would slay you for such opulence.
Your mission here among us peril fraught
Triumphant over death in our defence.
    Immortal bird with loving heart so pure,
    You give your life that others might endure.

ACKNOWLEDGEMENTS

Thank you to creative writing tutor Dave Copson for encouraging me in my writing and giving me the confidence to share it with others.

Thank you also Iain Lauchlan for believing in me and encouraging me to believe in myself

ABOUT CHERISH EDITIONS

Cherish Editions is a bespoke self-publishing service for authors of mental health, wellbeing and inspirational books.

As a division of Trigger Publishing, the UK's leading independent mental health and wellbeing publisher, we are experienced in creating and selling positive, responsible, important and inspirational books, which work to de-stigmatize the issues around mental health and improve the mental health and wellbeing of those who read our titles.

Founded by Adam Shaw, a mental health advocate, author and philanthropist, and leading psychologist Lauren Callaghan, Cherish Editions aims to publish books that provide advice, support and inspiration. We nurture our authors so that their stories can unfurl on the page, helping them to share their uplifting and moving stories.

Cherish Editions is unique in that a percentage of the profits from the sale of our books goes directly to leading mental health charity Shawmind, to deliver its vision to provide support for those experiencing mental ill health.

Find out more about Cherish Editions by visiting cherisheditions.com or by joining us on:
Twitter @cherisheditions
Facebook @cherisheditions
Instagram @cherisheditions

ABOUT SHAWMIND

A proportion of profits from the sale of all Trigger books go to their sister charity, Shawmind, also founded by Adam Shaw and Lauren Callaghan. The charity aims to ensure that everyone has access to mental health resources whenever they need them.

You can find out more about the work Shawmind do by visiting shawmind.org or joining them on:
Twitter @Shaw_Mind
Facebook @ShawmindUK
Instagram @Shaw_Mind

Shawmind
Your Local Mental Health & Wellbeing Charity

Lightning Source UK Ltd.
Milton Keynes UK
UKHW020623140322
400024UK00007B/201